The Caribou

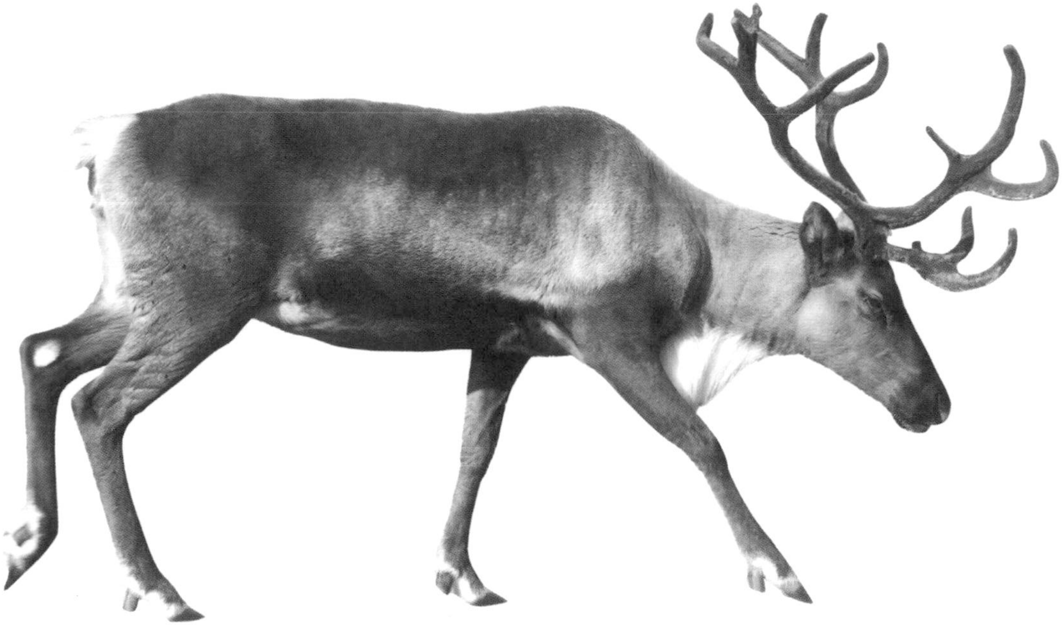

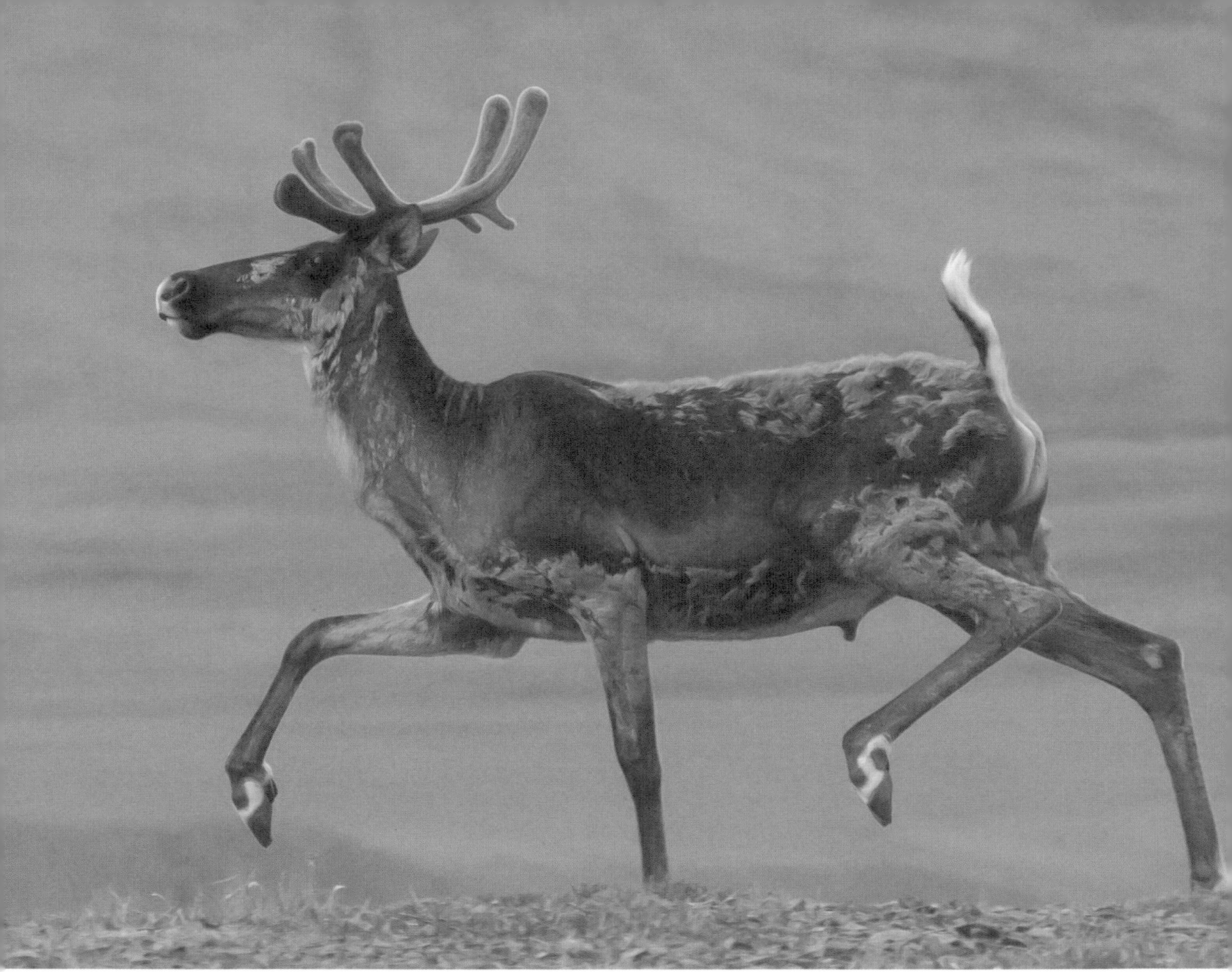

The caribou is running.

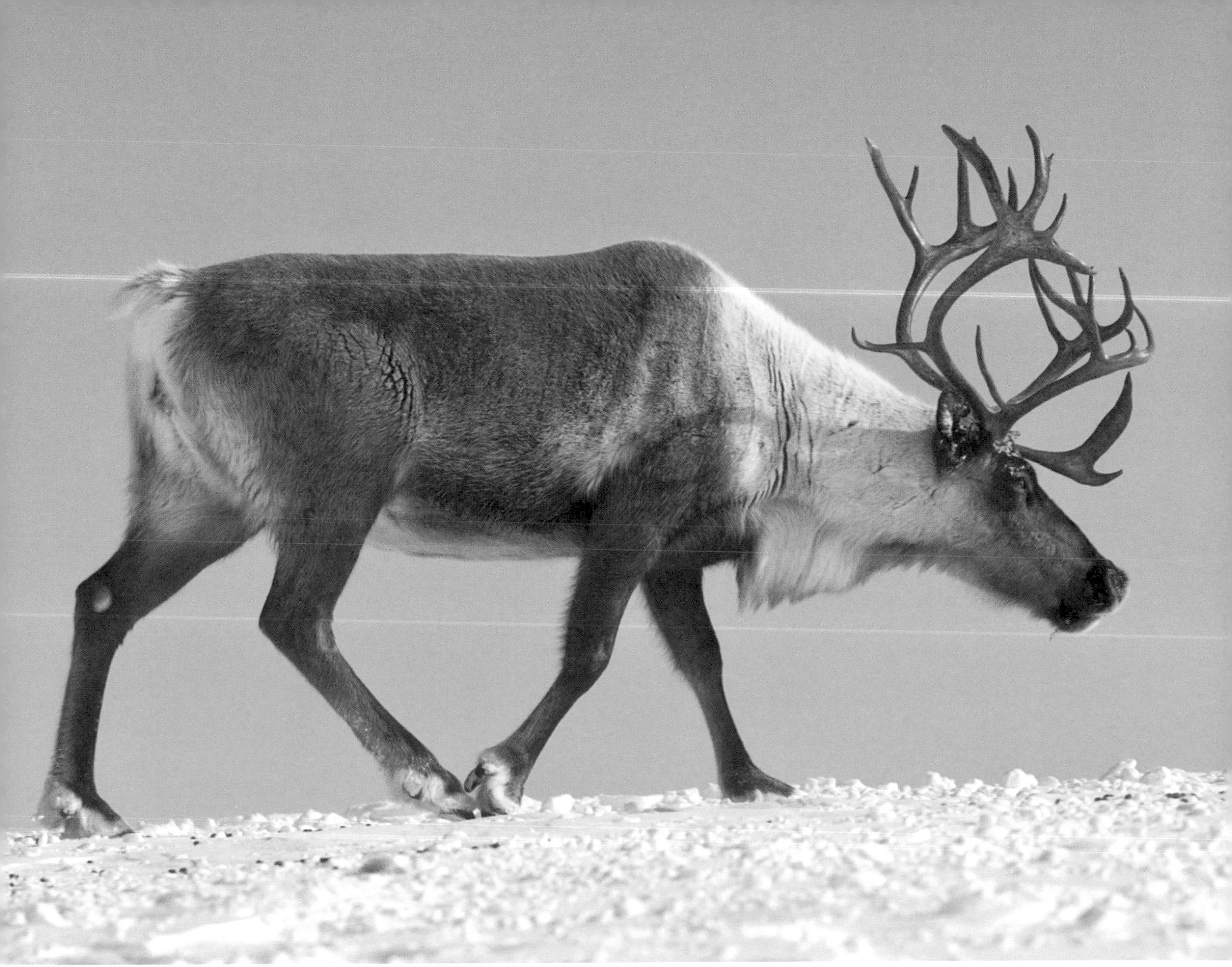

The caribou is walking.

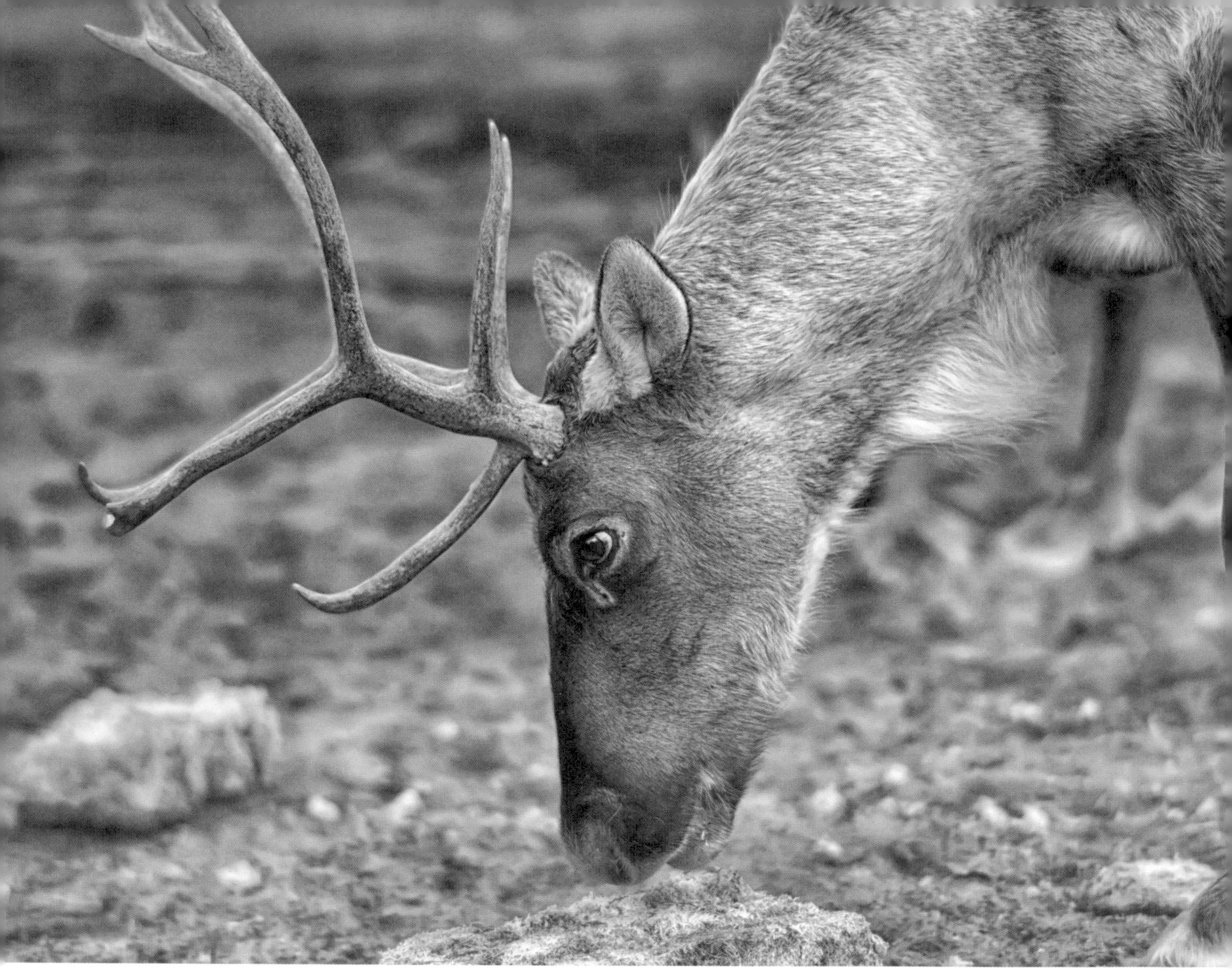

The caribou is eating.

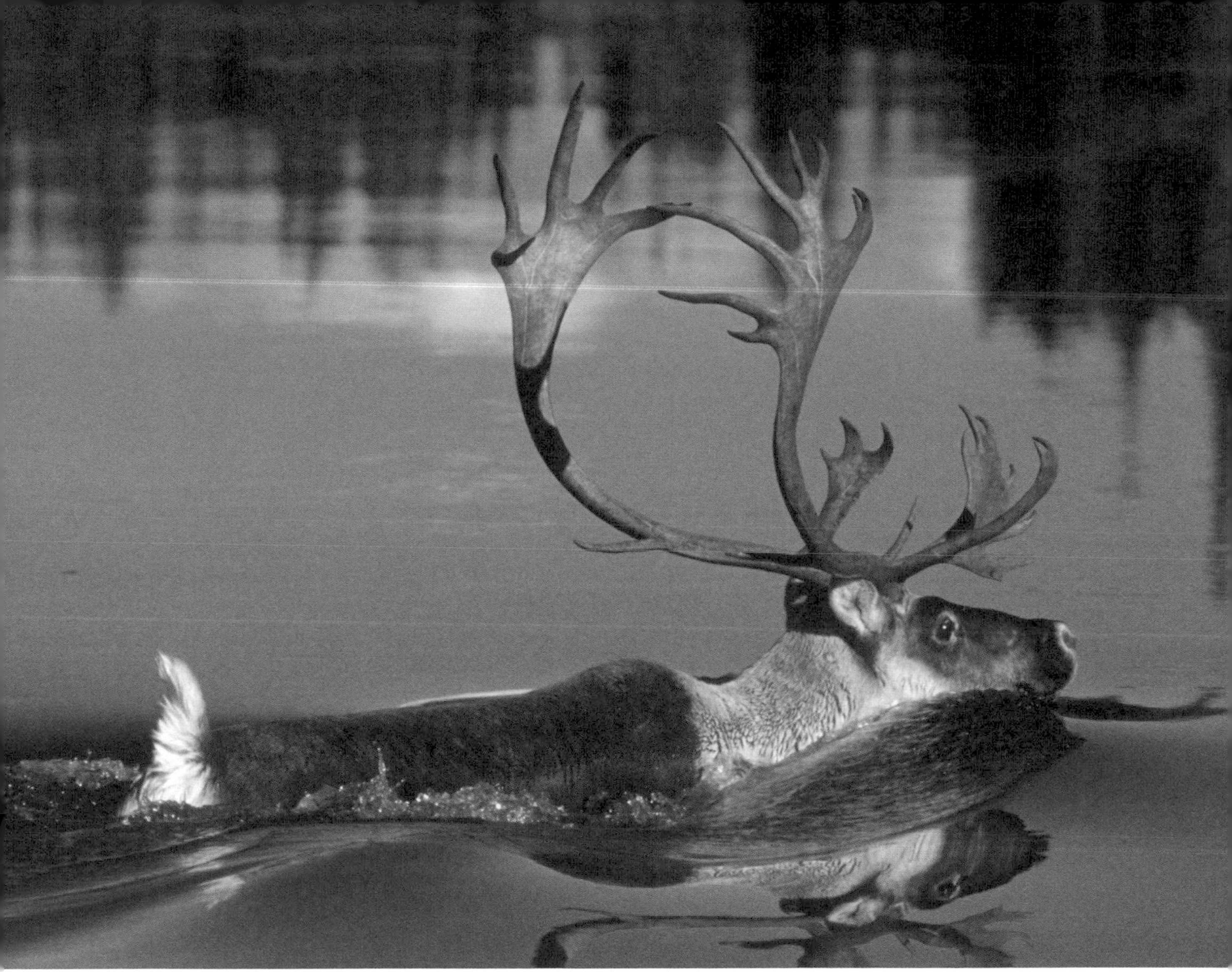

The caribou is swimming.

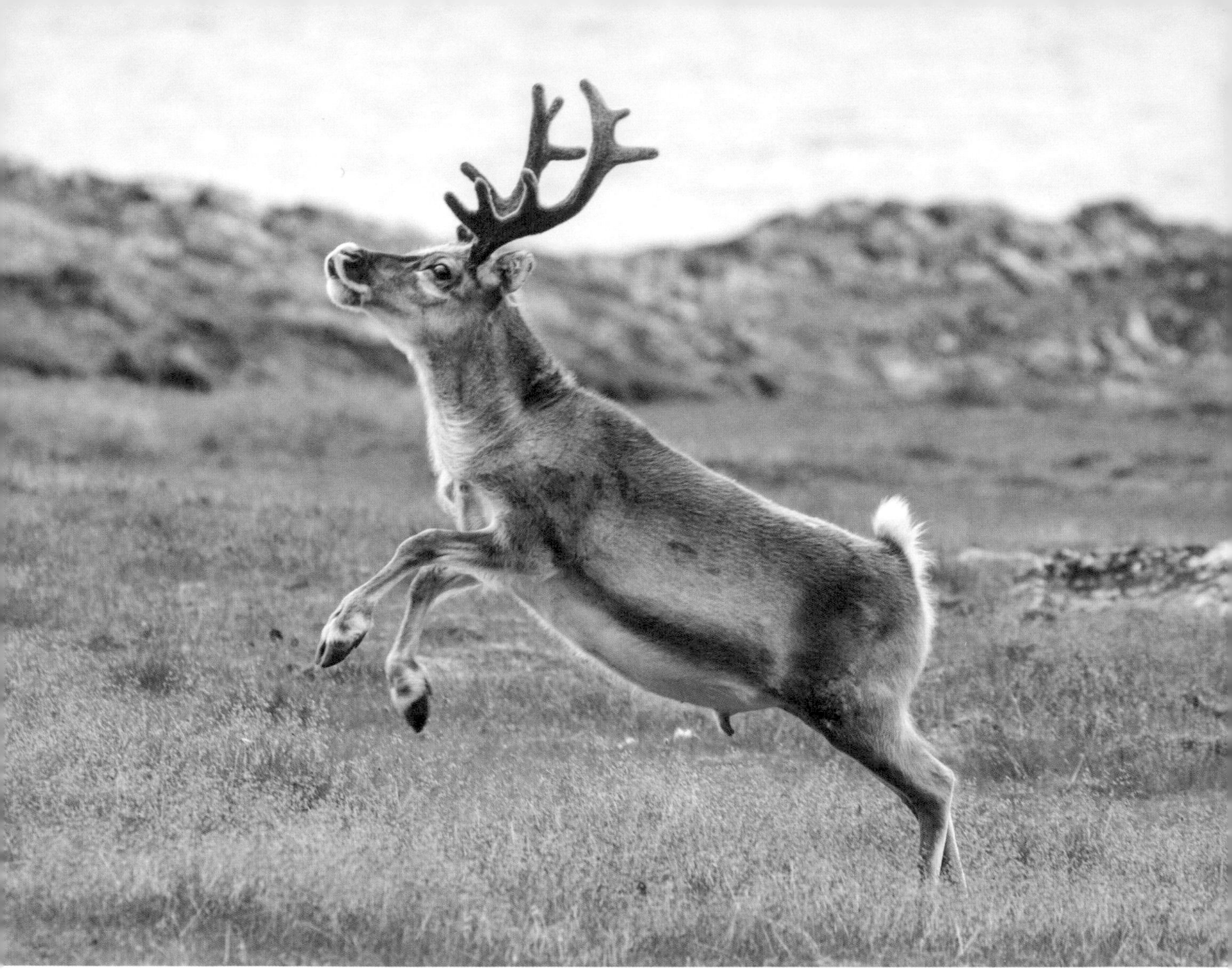

The caribou is jumping.

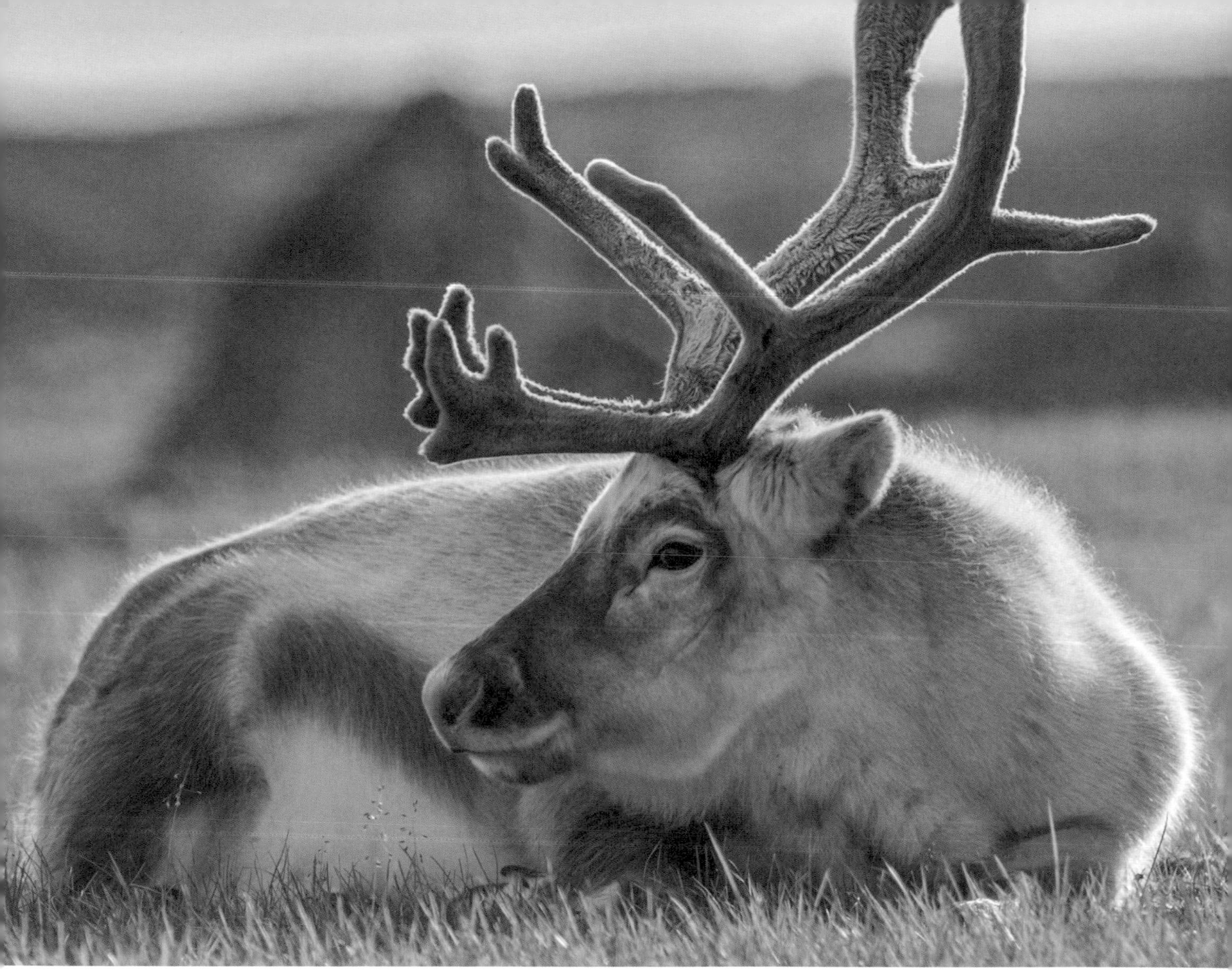

The caribou is resting.

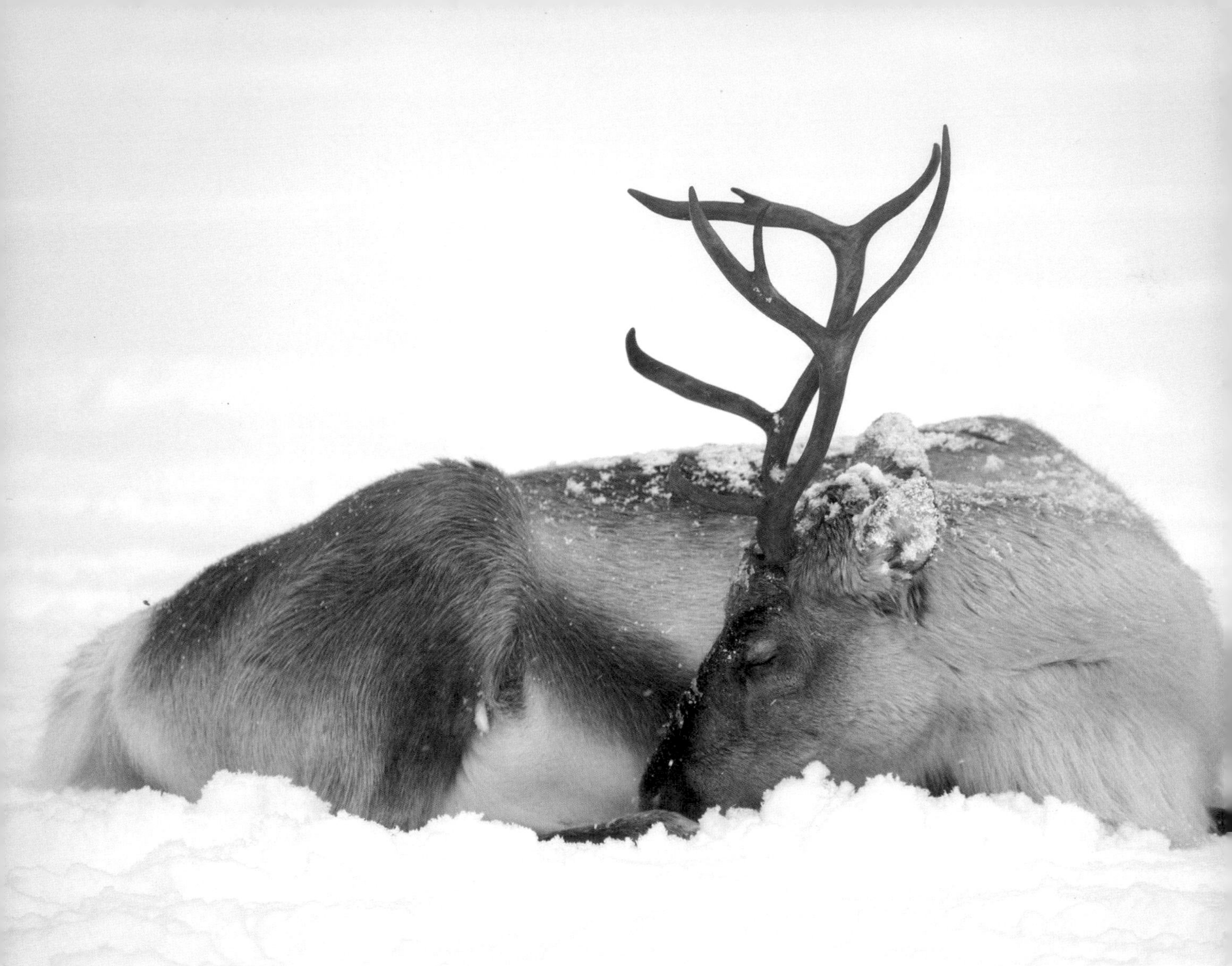

The caribou is sleeping.